Rome And Canterbury

A View From Geneva

A critique of the final report of the Anglican-Roman Catholic International Commission.

Donald Macleod

Christian Focus Publications Ltd.

Published by

Christian Focus Publications Ltd.

Tain   Houston
Ross-shire   Texas
Scotland   U.S.A.

© 1989 Christian Focus Publications Ltd.

ISBN 0906731 88 7

Christian Focus Publications is a non-denominational publishing house. We publish authors' books and the views expressed are those of the authors.

Contents

FOREWORD

I very warmly commend this book on the Anglican-Roman Catholic International Commission's Final Report to fellow Anglicans and, in particular, to members of the Church of England. I am glad that Professor Macleod has chosen to address himself to this subject, because his books and lectures are known for their clarity and penetration of thought, and he brings those qualities of mind to the examination of the ARCIC Statements. Those Statements present considerable difficulty to many church members, both lay and clergy, yet it is the duty of all to understand them and the nature of the 'agreement' which has been entered into on our behalf and endorsed by the General Synod and the Lambeth Conference. This book clears a way though the difficulty to reveal the wholly inadequate basis on which that agreement rests.

But there is another reason why this study of ARCIC is so valuable, and that is, that Professor Macleod brings an independent mind to the subject. He is a minister of the Free Church of Scotland, a Church which adheres to and upholds Reformed doctrines and principles — he describes his critique as 'A View from Geneva' — and he brings these doctrines and principles to bear upon the ARCIC Statements with great effect. Of course, substantially, the same Reformed teachings are to be found in the Thirty-Nine Articles of the Church of England; classical Anglicanism has much more in common with Geneva than it has with Rome. The tragedy today is that many have forgotten this. I hope that Professor Macleod's book will remind them, and also show them how those doctrines and principles must be applied to the life of the Church of England today, in order to reform it afresh. Perhaps the most poignant part of this analysis is where the author points out that, if ARCIC fails, it is likely to fail from some 'accident', such as the ordination of women, rather than because the Church of England understands itself and its essential nature and raison d'etre as a Reformed Church.

I hope that this book will enjoy a wide circulation and be read by many, for it not only reveals the weakness and defects of the ARCIC Statements in a most lucid manner; it also shows the need for Anglicans to affirm once again the true position and teaching of the Church of England.

David Samuel

PRIMACY AND UNITY

The current state of relations between the Church of England and the Roman Catholic Church is the result of work begun in January, 1967, when the Joint Preparatory Commission met at Gazzada in Italy. This meeting itself followed a joint decision by Pope Paul VI and Archbishop Michael Ramsay. Within a year the Preparatory Commission produced a Report which proclaimed 'penitence for the past, thankfulness for the graces of the present, urgency and resolve for a future in which our common aim would be the restoration of full organic unity' (*The Final Report*, p.1). The Report was endorsed 'in substance' by Cardinal Bea (then head of the Vatican's Secretariat for Unity) and by the 1968 Lambeth Conference.

The Anglican—Roman Catholic International Commission (which contained eight members of the original Preparatory Commission) first met in January, 1970. Its *Final Report* (which includes a large amount of previously published material) was published in 1982 and indicates that the Commission had three main areas of concern: the Eucharist, Ministry and Authority. A later Report, *Salvation and the Church* (often cited as *ARCIC II)* gave particular attention to the doctrine of justification.

The single most important issue in these discussions

has been the papal primacy. Its special significance was recognised by the Commission from the very beginning and the first of two Statements on Authority (*Authority in the Church*, 1976) acknowledged that 'it was precisely in the problem of the papal primacy that our historical divisions found their unhappy origin'. The question dominates the discussion of authority in *The Final Report* and it is frankly admitted that full visible communion cannot be achieved without the common acceptance of a universal primacy. More important, and more disturbing, is the calm, almost blasé, way the *Final Report* commits itself to recognition of the papal primacy as the only way forward: 'It seems appropriate that in any future union a universal primacy such as has been described should be held by that see' (p.64). Considering that centuries of history are being annulled, and the basic principles of our constitution challenged, such an announcement surely merited a little more sense of occasion.

The degree of agreement really is remarkable. There is no indication in *The Final Report* of any hesitation or tension within the commission: 'The only see which makes any claim to universal primacy and which has exercised and still exercises such *episkope* is the see of Rome, the city where Peter and Paul died. It seems appropriate that in any future union a universal primacy such as has been described should be held by that see..... What we have written here amounts to a consensus on authority in the Church and, in particular, on the basic principles of primacy' (p.64). There is an equally assured and unanimous statement on page 93: 'When matters of faith are at stake decisions may be made by the Church in universal councils; we are agreed that these are authoritative. We have also recognised the need in a united Church for a universal primate who, presiding over the *koinonia*, can speak with authority in the name of the Church.' No wonder that Hugh Montefiore, former Bishop of Birmingham, speaks of 'a truly amazing convergence of doctrine between Rome and Canterbury' (*So Near and Yet So Far* p.35).

Equally striking is the political register of the argument. The Vatican has clearly won its case and *The Final Report* becomes an exercise in selling the papal position. All that can be said for the Petrine primacy is said, but no attempt whatever is made to present the merits of Anglicanism. The arguments in favour of the Elizabethan settlement, whatever they are, have sunk without trace.

A Focus of Unity?

But what of the arguments actually presented?

The one on which *The Final Report* places most reliance is that the Church *needs* the kind of primacy offered by the Bishop of Rome. In particular, it needs a focus of unity. This is stated in various ways. We are told, for example, 'that in a reunited Church a ministry modelled on the role of Peter will be a sign and safeguard of unity' (p.85); or again, 'We have also recognised the need in a united Church for a universal primate who, presiding over the *koinonia*, can speak with authority in the name of the Church' (p.93); or, yet again, 'We can now together affirm that the Church needs both a multiple, dispersed authority, with which all God's people are actively involved, and also a universal primate as servant and focus of visible unity in truth and love' (p.98); or finally, 'According to Christian doctrine the unity in truth of the Christian community demands visible expression. We agree that such visible expression is the will of God and that the maintenance of visible unity at the universal level includes the *episkope* of a universal primate' (p.76).

The objections to such reasoning are formidable.

First, the assumption that the Church *needs* something is entirely gratuitous. It is for God to decide what His people need. The mere fact that we think something necessary is no guarantee that the Lord has provided it.

Secondly, the premises behind the argument are wrong. ARCIC is at pains to stress the conciliar nature of primacy. The Pope is the spokesman of the College of Bishops: 'A primate exercises his ministry not in isolation but in collegial association with his brother bishops' (p.63). He speaks in their name and expresses their mind. When these bishops meet in universal councils their decisions are authoritative. In fact, they are infallible: When the Church meets in ecumenical council its decisions on fundamental matters of faith exclude what is erroneous.' But what ground do we have for believing this? The New Testament knows nothing of 'bishops', even less of councils of 'bishops' and less still of *infallible* councils of 'bishops'. The Westminster Assembly surely spoke the truth: 'All synods or councils, since the Apostles' times, whether general or particular, may err; and many have erred. Therefore they are not to be made the rule of faith, or practice; but to be used as a help in both' (Chapter XXXI.IV). It would be very difficult for any Protestant to accept that the Council of Trent, for example, was infallible. In fact, there are clear signs within the documents produced by the International Commission itself that Roman Catholics are seriously embarrassed by the pronouncements of Trent, particularly those on the Eucharist and on Justification. God did not promise His church infallible conciliar authority; and He certainly has not granted it.

Thirdly, papal primacy does not in practice operate as *The Final Report* suggests. There the conciliar aspect is strongly emphasised: 'The primacy accorded to a bishop implies that, after consulting his fellow bishops, he may speak in their name and express their mind' (p.63). Later on, we read that the Bishop of Rome 'must speak explicitly as the focus within the *koinonia*; having sought to discover the mind of his fellow bishops and of the Church as a whole' (p.95). We shall examine this point more fully later. It will suffice for the moment to recall the wording of the Decree of Pope Pius IX on the Immaculate Conception of the Blessed Virgin Mary. The Decree (promulgated in 1854) speaks of the Pope 'imploring the protection of the whole celestial court' and 'invoking on our knees the Holy Ghost the Paraclete'. But it says nothing about consulting the 'other' bishops. What it says is this: '*We* pronounce, declare and define, by the authority of Our Lord Jesus Christ and the blessed Apostles Peter and Paul, *and in Our own authority,* that the doctrine which holds the Blessed Virgin Mary to have been, from the first moment of her conception, by a singular grace and privilege of almighty God, in view of the merits of Christ Jesus the

Saviour of all mankind, preserved free from all stain of original sin, was revealed by God, and is, therefore, to be firmly and constantly believed by all the faithful' (the italics are ours). There is no conciliarity here. There is only the confident affirmation of a man who sees himself as answering to no one on earth.

Fourthly, there is little reason to believe that the papal primacy has secured what its supporters claim for it. For example, according to *The Final Report,* 'A service of preserving the Church from error has been performed by the Bishop of Rome as universal primate' (p.94). It is also suggested (page 78) that the primacy has preserved Catholicism from 'doctrinal incoherence'. But neither claim is justified. The primacy did not prevent the gospel being betrayed at Trent. The truth, surely is, that papal supremacy is itself a tragic error; and that it has spawned a whole school of doctrines (notably the Marian dogmas) which have increasingly distanced Catholicism from the New Testament.

The claim that the primacy has prevented doctrinal incoherence fares no better. The Roman Catholic Church contains as much theological variety as any of the mainline Protestant denominations. It is still producing classic Tridentine theology: for example, Ludwig Ott's *Fundamentals of Catholic Dogma* (first published in English, 1955. 4th Edition re-issued, Illionois, 1974). But it is also producing the radical Christology of Edward Schillebeeckx (particularly *Jesus: An Experiment in Christology,* E.T. 1979) and the Liberation Theology of such men as Jon Sobrino (*Christology at the Crossroads: A Latin American View,* E.T. 1978). Catholicism has also produced its own tradition of iconoclastic biblical scholarship from Albert Loisy (1857-1940) to Raymond E. Brown, who in one of his recent publications declared, 'It can be claimed intelligently that most of the NT was written after the death of the last known apostle' (*The Churches the Apostles Left Behind,* New York, 1984). The distance between Ludwig Ott and such men is fully equal to that between Louis Berkhof and Paul Tillich. And we have not even mentioned Hans Kung, Karl Rahner and Yves Conger!

Historical argument

ARCIC also makes quite remarkable use of the historical argument for the papal primacy: the *de facto* situation that Rome is the only see which claims universal jurisdiction is regarded as a providential development brought about by the Holy Spirit. The only factor offered to reinforce this is that Rome is the city where Peter and Paul taught. By such logic, surely, the primacy should be located in Jerusalem, where *all* the apostles taught. The confident assumptions of ARCIC become all the more bizarre when we recall that *The Final Report* itself concedes that the weight traditionally put on the Petrine texts (especially Matt. 16.18) is greater than they can bear; recognises that the words spoken to Peter cannot be applied to the Bishop of Rome 'with an identical meaning'; and even questions the authenticity of the words themselves. To be met, after all this, with the argument that we must accept the primacy of the Pope because no one else claims such a primacy takes one's breath away. As Hugh Montefiore points out (*op cit.* p.46), 'Providence may express only the permissive will of God.' A thing is not right simply because it happened; nor true simply because it is claimed. The power and influence which Rome gathered to itself owed more to political intrigue than to the leading of the Spirit. If we are to absolutise history we may as well argue that Anglicanism emerged by divine providence and the restoration of the papacy would therefore be a grave act of collective impiety.

Less than honest

The overriding impression given by *The Final Report* is that in its portrayal of the papacy it is less than honest. It is at pains to represent the Pontiff as a benign, constitutional monarch, allowing other bishops a large measure of autonomy, never interfering in the internal affairs of their dioceses, always consulting them and functioning very much as a servant, never as a lord. The impression is conveyed, too, that the papal primacy is not terribly important to Romanism and that Catholicism takes a very liberal and tolerant view of Anglicanism's 16th century rejection of Vatican authority.

All this may suit Vatican diplomacy for the moment, but service, consultation and local autonomy are hardly prominent features in the portrait of the papacy drawn by official Catholic documents. In fact, the Roman Catholic bishops of England and Wales have already protested that the Agreed Statements of the International Commission give insufficient weight to the universal primacy, which they regard as of the very essence of the Church. Hugh Montefiore (himself a powerful advocate of closer relations between Anglicans and

Roman Catholics) has equally strong reservations. He regards the picture put forward by ARCIC as 'ideal' and adds: 'It differs in some important respects from the actual exercise of papal power as well as from the picture of the bishops, councils and papacy expressed in the Vatican II documents' (*op cit.* p.47).

This is a fair assessment. So far as Vatican II is concerned, the authority of the Pope is of a quite different order to that of the bishops, considered either singly or as a body. For one thing, 'The college or body of bishops has no authority unless united with the Roman Pontiff, Peter's successor, as its head' (*Dogmatic Constitution on the Church,* Chapter IIIa). Furthermore, the Pope in his own person, is Peter's successor and Vicar of Christ. As such, he has a primacy not only over the faithful in general but also over all other pastors: 'The Roman Pontiff has full, supreme and universal power over the whole Church, a power which he can always exercise unhindered' (*ibid*). In accordance with this, the papacy expects much greater respect and deference than the diplomatic language of ARCIC suggests. The teaching of the bishops is indeed to be received with 'a religious assent of the soul'. But, 'This religious submission of will and of mind must be shown in a special way to be the authentic teaching of the Roman Pontiff, even when he is not speaking *ex cathedra' (ibid)*. By *special* is meant *in such a way that 'his supreme magisterium is acknowledged with reverence and the judgements made by him are sincerely adhered to, according to his mind and intention' (ibid)*. The most intriguing thing about this statement is that the reverence it stipulates is to be accorded to papal teaching at all times, and not only on those occasions when he is officially exercising *his infallibility. This is what opponents of the encyclical Humanae Vitae* found to their cost. This pronouncement on sexual morality was not *ex cathedra* and yet the Vatican clearly tolerated no dissent from its teaching. In the event of union between Rome and Canterbury every Anglican priest would inevitably be bound by *Humanae Vitae*: and by every comparable papal utterance.

The picture of the papacy given by *The Final Report* also contradicts that given by the first Vatican Council. The Council's definition of papal infallibility is as follows:

'We teach and define that it is a dogma divinely revealed: that the Roman Pontiff, when he speaks *ex cathedra,* that is, when, in discharge of the office of pastor and teacher of all Christians, by virtue of his supreme Apostolic authority, he defines a doctrine regarding faith or morals to be held by the universal Church, is, by the divine assistance promised to him in Blessed Peter, possessed of that infallibility with which the divine Redeemer willed that His Church should be endowed in defining doctrine regarding faith or morals; and that, therefore, such definitions of the Roman Pontiff are of themselves, and not from the consent of the Church, irreformable.

But if anyone — which may God avert! — presume to change this our definition, let him be anathema.'

It is very interesting that this definition identifies the Pope so closely with 'the Blessed Peter'. An earlier statement in this same document (*The First Dogmatic Constitution on the Church of Christ*) is even more emphatic: 'We therefore teach and declare that, according to the testimony of the Gospel, the primacy of jurisdiction over the universal Church of

God was immediately and directly promised and given to Blessed Peter the Apostle by Christ the Lord.' This is in marked contrast to the tone of *The Final Report*, which, as we have seen, has a very cavalier attitude to the Petrine texts and denies that the words spoken to Peter can be applied to the papacy 'with an identical meaning'. There can be little doubt that once the dust of inter-church dialogue has settled the official dogmatic position of Rome will quickly reassert itself and the Vatican demand all the reverence due to 'the Blessed Peter'. Anglicanism will find itself in the belly of the whale.

Nor does Vatican I offer any hospitality to the idea of collegiality: 'Such definitions of the Roman Pontiff, of themselves — *and not by virtue of the consent of the Church* — are irreformable' (italics ours). Again, any ambiguity is dispelled by an earlier statement: 'At open variance with this clear doctrine of Holy Scripture, as it has ever been understood by the Catholic Church, are the perverse opinions of those who deny that Peter in his simple person preferably to all the other Apostles, whether taken separately or together, was endowed by Christ with a true and proper primacy of jurisdiction; or of those who assert that the same primacy was not bestowed immediately and directly upon Blessed Peter himself, but upon the Church, and through the Church on Peter as her minister.' The Pope of Vatican I is no mere colleague or servant.

Solid Core of Traditionalism

Inter-church dialogue is usually conducted by negotiators skilled in the trading of words. The Roman Catholic Church is well endowed with such men. But when their work is finished the solid core of Catholic traditionalism will take over. What this will mean for the role of the papacy in a united church can be seen far more clearly in Ludwig Ott's restatement of old-fashioned Catholicism than in such a communique as *The Final Report*. According to Ott (*The Fundamentals of Catholic Dogma,* pp. 276-291) the authority of Peter was such that all the other apostles, including Paul, were subordinate to him. This power was transmitted *simpliciter* to the Pope, who represents Christ on earth and functions as Supreme Head of the whole church. His power as such is awesome.

First, it is *universal.* The Pope has monarchical authority over every other bishop, who receives his power from him and exercises it as his subordinate. In effect, the Vatican has the same power over every diocese of the Church as it has over Rome.

Secondly, the papal power is *supreme:* 'There is no jurisdiction possessing a greater or equally great power. The power of the Pope transcends both the power of each individual bishop and also of all the other bishops together. The bishops collectively (apart from the Pope), therefore, are not equal to or superior to the Pope.' One result of this is that his holiness is not legally bound by ecclesiatical laws and usages: he answers to God alone. Another is that there can be no appeal to a higher court against the judgment of the Pope, 'because there is no higher judge on earth than he'.

Thirdly, the Primate possesses *full* power. He not only has more power than all the other bishops put together. He has *all* power: 'The Pope can rule independently on any matter which comes under the sphere of the Church's jurisdiction, without the concurrence of the other bishops or of the rest of the Church.'

Finally, papal power is *immediate*. The Pope can exercise his authority over any bishop, over any diocese and over any member of the faithful without going through any intermediary.

Of what value is ARCIC's talk of fellowship, collegiality, service and local independence in the face of such clear and passionate, dogmatic affirmations? None: especially when we recall that to the Pope himself (and to the vast majority of bishops and clergy) it is a sacred duty to protect and enhance the authority of the primacy. No college of cardinals could die in peace if it recognised the attenuated primacy of *The Final Report* as anything more than window-dressing: or bait.

POPE OR HOLY SPIRIT?

The basic assumption behind papal claims is that the departure of Christ from earth left a huge void in the church: a void which the ingenuity of later generations had to fill. This totally contradicts the Lord's own attitude to His return to His Father. It was with this very event in mind that He said to His disciples, 'Let not your hearts be troubled' (John 14.1). This was no empty exhortation. It was based on a solid, unambiguous promise, 'I will not leave you orphans. I will come again' (John 14.18). What exactly that meant was clarified later: 'it is good for you that I go away, for if I do not go away the Comforter will not come to you; but if I go away I will send him to you' (John 16.7). 'The fourth Gospel,' writes Oscar Cullmann, 'was written to show that in leaving the world Christ did not abandon it' (*The Early Church*, p.82). The Comforter would lead them into all truth. He would provide the focal point for Christian unity (John 17.21ff., Eph. 4.3). He would fully equip the people of God for their various ministries.

Unfortunately, the effects of these promises have not always been apparent in the actual life of the church. Leadership has too often fallen into the hands of unbelievers and been exercised in accordance with worldly power structures rather than according to the mind of the Spirit. But in the New Testament the effects of the Spirit's ministry are certainly dramatic enough. We see this most vividly in the story of

Pentecost where Peter's preaching, rooted in his experience of the Spirit, brings three thousand souls into the kingdom. But it was true throughout the New Testament period. The apostles, preaching in the power of the age to come, turned the world upside down. Ordinary Christians, filled with the Spirit, underwent radical personal transformation (Gal. 5.22f., 1 Cor. 6.11) and reached extraordinary heights of contentment and power (Eph. 5.19, Phil. 4.11,13).

Pentecost was virtually a parousia. It established the presence of Christ with His church for all time and made possible the fulfilling of His promise, 'I am with you all the days to the end of the world' (Matt. 28.20). In the light of it we are fully entitled to say that the Holy Spirit, not the Pope, is the Vicar of Christ.

It may be said, however, that this immediately creates the danger of subjectivism. Without a visible Head — without general councils, encyclicals and papal bulls — how can we know where we are? Will everyone not simply follow his own spirit? And will this not lead to total confusion?

The danger does indeed exist. Even in the seventeenth century, when the great Reformed confessions were drafted, there was a multiplicity of sects all claiming the guidance of the Holy Spirit. This is why the Westminster Confession, for example, warns against 'private spirits' (Chapter 1.10). Today the problem is still with us, probably in an even more acute form. On all sides there are Christian leaders making charismatic claims, announcing that they are prophets (or even apostles) and commanding the allegiance of multitudes.

The Canon Of Scripture

The immediate answer to this is that Christ has given us not only the Holy Spirit but also Holy Scripture. The church never existed without a Canon. At the beginning this consisted of the Old Testament scriptures and traces of the esteem in which these were held are clearly embedded in the apostolic writings. St Peter, for example, declares that these scriptures came into being not as a result of human insight and initiative but through the activity of the Holy Spirit; holy men spoke from God as they were carried by the Holy Spirit (2 Pet. 1.21). St Paul is equally clear. Every scripture, says he, is given by inspiration of God (literally, every scripture is 'God-breathed', 2 Tim. 3.16). Such an attitude to the Old Testament was rooted not in Rabbinism but in the teaching of the Lord Himself. He pointed friend and foe alike to these scriptures, appealing to them in support of His own teaching, drawing from them, to a large extent, His understanding of Himself and His mission and declaring categorically that they could not be broken (John 10.35).

The Spirit In The Church

But from the beginning of the church something else was happening, too: this Canon was being augmented. For one thing, there was the teaching of the Lord Himself, understood from the very beginning as 'commandments' (Matt. 28. 20) and making such an impression even on outsiders that they commented that He 'taught as one having authority and not as the scribes' (Matt. 7. 29). After the

Ascension, this expansion of the Canon continued through the teaching of the apostles. As early as Acts 2.42 we see the early Christians gathering eagerly to be taught by the Eleven. Obviously this was oral teaching but the respect accorded to it is clear from such a passage as 1 Thes. 2. 13. Paul's hearers received his word not as the word of men but as the word of God. By this time the Canon was already becoming complex: the Old Testament, the recollected teaching of the Lord and the preaching of the apostles. The final stage came when the teaching of the Lord and the apostles was put in written form in the four gospels and in the various other documents which we know today as the New Testament. Putting them in written form did not make the teaching any more authoritative. Indeed, it was not even absolutely necessary. Reformed theology has certainly insisted that *revelation* was absolutely necessary. But it regarded the writing down of that revelation as a luxury. It is part of the extravagance of grace, given to us 'for the *better* preserving and propagating of the truth and for the *more sure* establishment and comfort of the church' (Westminster Confession, I.I).

From the earliest days these apostolic writings (both gospels and epistles) were regarded as scripture and put on a par with the Old Testament. For example, in 1 Tim. 5.18, Paul reinforces the idea that the elders who rule well are to be accounted worthy of double remuneration by appealing to two 'scriptures'. One is from Deut. 25.4, 'You shall not muzzle the ox when it is treading grain.' The other is from the Gospel of Luke: 'The labourer deserves his wages' (Luke 10.7). Paul clearly regards both these sources as equally authoritative. We find a similar situation in 2

Peter where the apostle rebukes those who abuse the Pauline letters 'as they do the other scriptures' (2 Pet. 3.16). This categorical endorsement leaves no room for ambiguity. Paul's epistles, so far as Peter is concerned, belong to that category of writings which came not by private interpretation but by the initiative of God the Holy Spirit (2 Pet. 1. 20f.). Besides, these writings are not merely *records* of revelation. They are real, living revelation. In them the church still enjoys the ministry of apostles and prophets, speaking to us with the utmost directness in the pages of the New Testament.

But we enjoy more. We enjoy the on-going ministry of the risen Christ. This is as true of the epistles as it is of the gospels, because of the very nature of the New Testament idea of *tradition*. The apostles (especially Paul) saw their teaching ministry as part of a complex process of giving and receiving. They received their message from Christ; and they passed it on authoritatively to their hearers and readers. We see this reflected in, for example, Gal. 1.11: 'The gospel which was preached by me is not man's gospel. For I did not receive it from man, nor was I taught it, but it came through a revelation of Jesus Christ.' Paul expresses similar sentiments in 1 Cor. 11.23ff in connection with his teaching on the Lord's Supper: 'I received from the Lord what I also delivered to you......'. 1 Cor. 15. 3, 4 expresses the idea even more completely: 'I delivered to you as of first importance what I also received, that Christ died for our sins in accordance with the scriptures, that he was buried, that he was raised on the third day according to the scriptures and that he was seen.'

Such statements fully justify Cullmann's claim that

'the exalted Lord is the real author of the whole tradition developing itself within the apostolic Church. For in Christ alone can there be a tradition which is not a "tradition of men"' (*The Early Church*, pp. 62, 66). In fact, the giving of the tradition belongs to the series of redemptive acts performed by the Lord for the church, so that Cullmann is again quite correct when he says that 'the apostolate does not belong to the period of the Church but to that of the incarnation' (*op. cit., p. 78*). The risen Lord is present and active in the apostolic pronouncements, even in those which relate to apparently non-central issues such as women speaking in church. Paul gives his views on this in 1 Cor. 14. 32-40 and concludes, 'If anyone thinks that he is a prophet, or a spiritual man, he should acknowledge that the things I am writing to you are the commandments of the Lord'.

Scripture And The Spirit

But there is something else which it is vital not to overlook: the connection between scripture and the Holy Spirit. It is as true of the written as of the spoken word that it comes 'in demonstration of the Spirit'. In fact the New Testament probably could not tolerate any very firm distinction between the work of the risen Christ in this area and the work of the Holy Spirit. This appears with particular clarity in the Epistles to the Seven Churches (*Rev. 2.1-3.22*). The introduction of each of these refers to Christ as their author. They come from 'the one who holds the seven stars in his right hand, who walks among the seven golden lampstands'. But the conclusion points equally clearly to the Spirit: 'He who has an ear, let him hear what the

Spirit says to the churches.' Clearly there is no difference between saying, 'Thus says the Lord!' and saying, 'Thus says the Spirit!'.

This is vital to our understanding of the ministry of the Holy Spirit as the Vicar of Christ. He never leads us *against* scripture. He leads us by means of it. This includes the fact that the Spirit is the One who interprets scripture, although the point has to be made at once that He does not do this autonomously or unilaterally. He uses the ministry of human interpreters who are called by Him, endowed with the requisite gifts and guided and upheld as they go about their work. The importance of this is reflected in the Ethiopian Chancellor's response to Philip's question in Acts 8.30, 'Do you understand what you read?'. 'How can I,' came the reply, 'unless someone guides me?'. But there is also a ministry of the Spirit in the hearts of the hearers and readers of the Word. He opens our hearts, removing our prejudices and overcoming our human aversion to the truth. He keeps us from 'wresting' the scriptures, bending and twisting them to suit our own purposes. Above all, He gives us the proper perspective, enabling us to approach the Word on its own terms and to see things from God's point of view.

Roman Catholic Protest

Precisely at this point, however, there is a well articulated protest from Roman Catholicism. Classic Catholic theology distinguishes between the *rule* and the *judge*. The Bible, it says, may be the rule: but who is the judge? Who is to tell what constitutes scripture, what scripture means and how its teaching applies in our current situation? The answer, according to Catholicism, is: the Church. This is probably the main reason why Roman Catholic theologians are so fond of maximising the difficulties involved in interpreting the Bible and why it has been so happy to align itself with radical schools of biblical criticism (despite its official commitment to a high doctrine of inspiration). The greater the obscurity, the more inadequate the scriptures and the greater the complexities of biblical scholarship the greater the need for the judge.

How this works in practice can be seen in Bullough's *Roman Catholicism*. Bullough's starting-point is a quotation from Thomas Aquinas: 'The truth of the faith is spread abroad in the Sacred Scriptures in many various forms, some of them very obscure, so that the task of extracting the truth of the faith from Sacred Scripture is one which requires long study and practice' (page 17). From this, several momentous conclusions follow.

First, there is a need for an interpretation of scripture which is at once authoritative, clear, confident and unanimous. 'There can be no question of divided or conflicting voices proclaiming the teaching of Christ,' writes Bullough: 'If the trumpet give an uncertain sound, who shall prepare himself to the battle?' (*op. cit.*, p. 163).

Secondly, after the age of the gospel, this authority had to be vested in a human organisation, which 'arrives at its conclusions by study, discussion and sometimes dispute, trusting meanwhile that the Holy Spirit will not allow error to penetrate' (*ibid*).

Thirdly, the Roman Catholic Church *is* this organisation and possesses this teaching authority 'in virtue of Christ's promises to the apostles and to Peter in particular, and His assurance that He would be with them even to the consummation of the age' (*ibid*).

Fourthly, precisely because it is a human organisation, the Church must have a human head upon earth and this head must be able 'to decide and teach with Christ's authority and infallibility or immunity from error' (*op. cit.*, p.164).

What we have here is a series of gratuitous assumptions. Why must there be an infallible interpreter? Why should we believe that the Church of Rome (rather than the Church of Stornoway) is this infallible interpreter? And why must such an organisation have one human head? Bullough does not tell us. But one thing is clear: The dogmatic position of the Church of England is quite irreconcilable with such imperialism and self-aggrandisement on the part of the Church of Rome: 'As the Church of Jerusalem, Alexandria and Antioch have erred; so also the Church of Rome hath erred, not only in their living and manner of Ceremonies, but also in matters of Faith' (*Articles of Religion,* XIX). The Articles also refuse to speak of the church as a judge and will allow only that it is 'a witness and keeper of holy writ' (XX). The church itself has to live under the judgment of scripture: 'It is not lawful for the Church to ordain any thing that is contrary to God's Word written, neither may it so expound one place of Scripture, that it be repugnant to another.' These limitations, according to the Articles, apply to General Councils as much as to other ecclesiastical gatherings: 'They may err, and sometimes have erred, even in things pertaining to God. Wherefore things ordained by them as necessary to salvation have neither strength nor authority, unless it may be declared that they be taken out of Holy Scripture' (XXI). It is impossible to graft such an outlook on to the stock of Catholicism; or to satisfy the expectations of Rome while safeguarding the integrity of Anglicanism. The two approaches differ root and branch: so much so, in fact, that it can be argued that they represent two entirely different religions.

The idea of the church as judge is taken up explicitly in the Westminster Confession (I.X): 'The supreme Judge, by which all controversies of religion are to be determined, and all decrees of councils, opinions of ancient writers, doctrines of men, and private spirits, are to be examined, and in whose sentence we are to rest, can be no other but the Holy Spirit speaking in the scripture.' The intention here was not to draw a distinction between *scripture* speaking and the *Holy Spirit* speaking but to assert that it is in scripture the Spirit speaks. This again assumes that scripture is not merely an inert record of a once vibrant revelation. It speaks; and in it the Spirit speaks. All merely human pronouncements are subject to Him, whether they come from the Fathers, General Councils or the Vatican. If what these say lacks biblical warrant it cannot bind any human conscience. In fact, the only way the Pope himself can know the truth is from scripture. What is more, the only way he can know the meaning of scripture is from scripture: 'the infallible rule of interpretation of scripture is the scripture itself; and therefore, when there is any question about the true and full sense of scripture (which is not manifold, but one), it must be searched out and known by other places that speak more clearly' (Westminster Confession, I.IX).

The Roman Catholic response to this is that it plunges us into uncertainty. Father Ronald Knox, for example, alleges that mere study of the Bible 'is humanly certain to lead different men to different conclusions even on subjects of the highest moment' (*The Belief of Catholics,* p.138). He cites as examples two modern questions: Can Christian marriage be dissolved? And, is there eternal punishment beyond the grave for impenitent sinners? The Bible does not give a clear answer on either of these, he argues, and therefore it is impossible for Protestantism to offer a united front to men's eager questioning.

Do We Need Expert Guidance?

But scripture is not at all as ambiguous as the Catholic argument suggests and it is simply mischievous to claim that without expert guidance ordinary Christians can make nothing of it. The Reformers quite rightly made the perspicuity of scripture a major part of their message. The Westminster Confession is typical: 'All things in scripture are not alike plain in themselves, nor alike clear unto all; yet those things which are necessary to be known, believed, and observed for salvation, are so clearly propounded in some place of scripture or other, that not only the learned, but the unlearned, in a due use of the ordinary means, may attain unto a sufficient understanding of them' (I.VIII).

This statement recognises that there are obscure passages in the Bible. One thinks immediately of Rev. 20, 1-10 and 1 Pet. 3,18-22. There are also certain doctrines (such as the millennium) on which the Bible's teaching is far from clear and on which, therefore, Christians have been unable to agree. But the doctrines we need to know are revealed with crystal clarity: the deity of Christ, vicarious atonement, the necessity of the new birth, the second coming, the fundamental principles of conduct. Not that every biblical statement on these doctrines is easily understood. But taking the Bible as a whole there are sufficient clear and unambiguous statements to place the overall teaching beyond dispute. Nor is this teaching accessible only to the expert biblical scholar ('the learned', as the Confession calls them). The clarity is such that even the 'unlearned' can get a perfectly adequate grasp of them. To do so they need not the guidance of an infallible church or the 'unanimous consent of the Fathers' or some special revelation. What they need is a 'due use of the ordinary means'. These include what are called Bible study aids: dictionaries, concordances, lexicons and commentaries. But their primary reference is to what Protestantism called 'the means of grace' and particularly to preaching. Through prayer, fellowship and preaching the humblest believer can become proficient in the truth. This is what William Tyndale meant when he vowed that if God spared him 'every boy that driveth the plough should know the scriptures'.

Yet this is never an autonomous human achievement, far less a merely intellectual one. The Word is effective only in conjunction with the Spirit: 'We acknowledge the inward illumination of the Spirit of God to be necessary for the saving understanding of such things as are revealed in the word' (Westminster Confession I.VI). Some understanding of biblical truth is possible apart from the Spirit's ministry, but there can be no *saving* understanding unless He works in our hearts. Equally, however, the combination of this ministry and the Bible's own perspicuity means that the believer is not beholden to any human institution when seeking to learn God's mind from the scriptures. The Bible is the book of the laity: the book of the people of God. They must have it in their own language ('the vulgar tongue'). They must be told that every page in it was meant for *them* and, with the Spirit's help, is within their grasp. And they must be urged to read it and to search it so that 'through patience and comfort of the scriptures they may have hope'. Anything which erects barriers between the people and the Book is to be condemned. God breathed out the scriptures (2 Tim. 3.16) so that *the man of God* (the ordinary Christian, not the priest or the expert biblical scholar) might become perfect.

On the other hand, where the Bible is ambiguous why not live with the ambiguity? Father Knox appears to imply that all uncertainty is evil. The real evil is to pretend to be certain where there are no grounds for certainty: The secret things belong to the Lord. Only those things which are revealed belong to us and to our children (Deut. 29.29). It is, of course, extremely irritating to the enquiring mind that there should be secret things. But such is undoubtedly the case. The Bible has no answer to the question, are they few that be saved? — Or to the question, how can we reconcile divine foreordination and human responsibility? Or to many others. Any answers to such questions, no matter how self-assured, can never be other than speculative.

The same is true in connection with many complex, albeit urgent, ethical questions. The Bible, in the last analysis, has nothing to say on contraception. Nor does it give us any moral ready-reckoner to provide quick and easy answers to complex questions of divorce and marital tension. Nor again does it come up with clear answers to the dilemmas posed by bio-ethics. When does humanness (or the right to brotherly protection) begin? At conception, is the safest answer. But when is conception? At the moment of fertilisation, when the sperm and ovum fuse? Or at the moment of implantation, when the fertilised ovum attaches itself to the wall of the uterus? There may be answers to such questions. But they are not biblical answers. They can never have the status of revealed truth: and the church certainly does not have the right to preface them with, 'Thus saith the Lord!'.

How can the Pope himself be certain where the Bible is not certain? He has every right to form a personal judgment, reflecting his own understanding of the evidence. But such a judgment binds only his own conscience and behaviour. It is totally irrelevant to anyone else. His pronouncements are authoritative only if they carry the support of scripture and he can convince our consciences that they do so. Even an apostle had to recognise that if he proclaimed novelties for which there was no canonical support his message should be rejected: 'Though we, or an angel from heaven, preach any other gospel unto you than that which we have preached to you, let him be accursed. As we said before, so say I now again, If any man preach any other gospel to you than that ye have received, let him be accursed' (Gal. 1.8,9). Personal prestige counted for nothing if the message was 'other' than what had already been received.

Catholic Tensions

Father Knox's comments highlight a fundamental difference between Protestant and Catholic psychology. Protestantism is prepared to live with uncertainties and to tolerate theological variety. Its whole instinct is to limit the number of items imposed as matters of faith. It encourages individuals to use their own judgment and to tolerate the different opinions of others. The traditional Catholic mind, by contrast, wants certainty and uniformity. All questions must be answered. Official statements must be provided, defining 'the Church's view'. The faithful must be guided by an unceasing flood of encyclicals, decrees and papal pronouncements. Hence the dogmatic, binding statements on questions the Bible would never even ask: Was the Virgin conceived immaculately? Hence, too, the totally non-biblical teaching on contraception.

At one level this is no more than an abuse of ecclesiastical authority. Such authority, as defined by our Lord, is only ministerial. It has no right to make rules but only to ascertain those laid down by Christ and administer them on His behalf. In practice this means that the church's pronouncements are authoritative only if supported by the Word of God, Holy Scripture.

But on another level, there is no doubt that 'the people love to have it so'. Being a mature child of God, standing on one's own two feet, cultivating one's own relationship with the Father, praying for ourselves and searching God's word for ourselves: all this can be exceedingly demanding, even traumatic. Many Christians wish, albeit unconsciously, that they were back in the womb, or at least that they were children again. Then someone could lead them by the hand and tell them what to do and protect them from all the terrible questions.

This was the very situation that led Paul to implore the Galatians to 'stand fast in the freedom with which Christ had made them free' (Gal. 5.1). They wanted to be minors again: even to be slaves. That would take away the agonies of maturity, decision-making and personal responsibility. There would be clear orders, specific beliefs and detailed moral guidelines. In the last twenty years this mentality has come under threat even within Roman Catholicism itself. Vatican II encouraged the laity to take a greater part in the life of the church and specifically to engage in Bible Study for themselves. But whether the change of direction is permanent remains to be seen. The papal primacy by its very nature creates intellectual and spiritual dependence, and if the laity become too mature and too adult the Vatican will not hesitate to remind them that they are only children and that Mother Church knows best.

Yet the Roman Catholic Church is nothing like as unanimous as its apologists claim. The tensions are obvious. Augustine and Aquinas had radically different approaches to the question of the knowledge of God; Aquinas and Anselm both denied the notion of the Immaculate Conception; Janenists and Jesuits were poles apart in their views of sin, grace and predestination; and at the moment Pope John Paul and Archbishop Lefebvre seem quite irreconcilable. It is very difficult to convince an outside observer that the Council of Trent and Vatican II present a united front; or indeed that Vatican I and Vatican II present a united front. Modern Roman Catholic scholars (including those involved in ARCIC) betray clear signs of stress as they try to explain (or explain away) the teaching of Trent on transubstantiation and on the re-presentation of Christ's offering in the sacrifice of the Mass. Who could harmonise Conger and Ott? Or even Newman and Wiseman?

The lack of unanimity becomes intriguingly clear if we compare the Syllabus of Errors (published in 1864) with subsequent developments in the Roman Catholic Church. That Syllabus condemned virtually every aspect of the contemporary intellectual life of Europe. It condemned toleration. It condemned the idea that there was some hope of salvation for those who were not Catholics. It condemned the idea that Protestantism was an authentic form of the Christian religion. It condemned Liberalism, Socialism, Bible Societies and biblical criticism. A hundred years later, the Second Vatican Council endorsed virtually everything the Syllabus had condemned. Today Roman Catholic scholars are in the forefront of biblical criticism and Latin American priests are formulating a political theology only a hair's breadth removed from Marxism.

The united front is an illusion. One age of the church contradicts another. One doctor contradicts another. One province contradicts another. Once we move out of a very limited area (dogmas the Roman Catholic Church shares with the rest of Christendom) we hear only a babble of conflicting voices.

Infallibility

The Roman Catholic response to this is that the Church's infallibility (and hence unanimity) is strictly limited. It applies only to pronouncements made *ex cathedra*, with a view to binding the consciences of all the faithful, and on matters which must be believed for salvation.

To which we must reply that it is surely very strange (and very sad) that an institution gifted with infallibility should use its gift so infrequently: and on issues so peripheral to men's 'eager questioning' (to use Knox's phrase). The Pope was declared (or discovered) to be infallible in 1870 but the benefit of this to mankind has been negligible. A great deal of the available insight has been used up defining what infallibility means and how it works; and what little energy is left has gone into pronouncements on questions in which most human beings have not the remotest interest. His holiness has spoken *ex cathedra* only once: and then only to declare that the body of the Virgin Mary was taken up to heaven immediately after her death. What matters at the moment is not whether these doctrines are true but whether such a use of infallibility is sound economics: or at least whether it reflects a due sense of pastoral proportion.

Infallibility is not a commodity to be squandered. Father Knox spoke of men's 'eager questioning' and boasted that his church — and his church alone — had the answers. But where are the answers? The modern Christian might welcome an infallible commentary on Holy Scripture but so far we haven't had an infallible exegesis of one single verse. He might welcome, too, an infallible exposition of Christian doctrine. It has not been forthcoming. We haven't even had an infallible definition of transubstantiation (or of infallibility, for that matter). Today's believer cries out for guidance on such questions as nuclear warfare and capital punishment. He asks, is AIDS the judgment of God? But the one infallible institution in the world says nothing. Or, if it does speak, it prefaces its remarks by saying, This is not one of my infallible utterances. Even on the issue of contraception it has refused to speak infallibly.

No united front, then, and no infallible answers to the questions that really matter. But there is a deeper issue still. Suppose it to be true that we need an infallible guide and that that guide is the church: How can we be sure that the Roman Catholic Church is that church? As we have seen, the ARCIC arguments for recognising the Roman primacy amount to little more than saying that Rome claims it, no one else claims it, so let Rome have it. This is hardly enough. It may indeed be true that no one else claims infallibility. But is it not possible that this is only because they have more sense? And anyway it is a fact, equally providential, that many dispute Rome's claims; and if providence is to be our guide we may as well be guided by this fact as by the other. The Eastern Church rejects these claims. Protestants reject them. Muslims reject them. Hans Kung rejects them in the name of Liberal Catholicism, and Archbishop Lefebvre rejects them in the name of traditional Catholicism. And there are good reasons for rejecting them. The infallible guide has too often been incoherent, muddled and self-contradictory. It has been guilty of monumental blunders, such as the condemnation of Galileo and Luther. And its *modus operandi* has been passing strange, the *ex cathedra* pronouncements looking suspiciously like opportunist reactions to mounting pressure from the faithful.

We must press the matter further. The lynch-pin of Rome's argument is that without an infallible guide we cannot have certainty. To which a Protestant might nod instant agreement and point to his infallible Bible. But ah! says Rome, You cannot do that! How do you know your Bible is infallible in the first place? You can only be sure of that if the infallible Church tells you. 'What authority have we,' asks Knox triumphantly, 'to say that the Epistles of Paul are inspired, and the Epistle of Barnabas is not' (*op. cit.*, p.136). But we cannot escape from the circle of uncertainty simply by appealing to the authority of the church. That only pushes the question one step further back: What authority do we have for believing in the infallibility of the church? Precious little! As William Cunningham pointed out in one of his notes to Stillingfleet's *Doctrines and Practices of the Church of Rome* (1845, page 185) every argument used by Roman Catholicism to prove that there must be an infallible interpreter of scripture 'equally proves the necessity of a statement distinctly asserting that the Church, and the Church of Rome, has been invested with that office........... The right of the Church of Rome to interpret infallibly the Scriptures must be founded upon the express testimony of God, else it cannot be received: and as no such testimony can be produced, the pretended right of that Church to interpret Scripture has, in point of fact, just as completely failed in guiding men to correct and harmonious views of God's revealed will as the exercise of private judgment'.

The only remotely plausible argument used by Roman Catholicism to buttress its case is taken from the words of our Lord in Matt. 16.19: 'And I will give unto thee the keys of the kingdom of heaven; and whatsoever thou shalt bind on earth shall be bound in heaven; and whatsoever thou shalt loose on earth shall be loosed in heaven.' The journey from these words to the notion of papal infallibility is, so far as logic goes, a long one. *Thee* and *the Pope* are not self-evidently identical. But the real issue is this: are we not now using scripture to buttress the authority of the Church? And does that not bring us right back into the circle: How do we know the scriptures are correct?

The Witness of The Spirit

On the premises of pure rationalism there is no way out of this circle. Our final authority cannot be validated by some other authority (logic, rational argument) without ceasing to be our final authority. Protestant confidence in the scriptures is not, in the last analysis, simply a form of rationalism. It rests on the witness of the Spirit. That witness is not, of course, irrational. The Spirit uses arguments and evidences; especially the testimony of the church to the value of scripture and the Bible's own internal evidence of its divine origin. But our confidence at last is not simply rational. It is spiritual: which means Spiritual. We end up with an intellectual peace which passes all understanding (Phil. 4.7). To ask for further vindication and proof of this really means asking, how can we be sure the Holy Spirit is right? The question is both impossible and improper. The Spirit produced the book. He stamped His character on it. He witnesses to it, making us sensitive to its heavenliness and creating a deep inner impulse to the assurance that it comes from God. The spiritual man hearing the apostles preach knew that their word came from God. The spiritual man reading the apostles' writings knows that they come from God. We cannot appeal beyond that for confirmation (although we can keep on arguing that the Bible is God's Word and hope the Spirit will give our arguments force). As Paul reminded the Thessalonians, the gospel came to them not in word only but also in power and in the full persuasiveness of the Spirit (1 Thes. 1.5). As a result they received it not as the word of men but as the word of God (1 Thes. 2.13). This is the background to his great boast in Rom. 1.16 that the gospel was God's power. Truth had its own force and the gospel carried all prejudice and blindness before it, testifying to itself and creating the faith it demanded. From the very beginning Protestantism grasped this clearly. We find a typical statement in George Gillespie: 'The Scripture is known to be indeed the Word of God by the beams of divine authority which it hath in itself, and by certain distinguishing characters, which do infallibly prove it to be the Word of God; yet all these cannot beget in the soul a full persuasion of faith that the Scriptures are the Word of God; this persuasion is from the Holy Spirit in our hearts' (*A Treatise of Miscellany Questions,* Chapter XXI).

It would be quite wrong, however, to go away with the impression that Protestant exegesis of the scriptures is simply a matter of private judgment, as if the individual did his own thing and ignored the insights of the universal church. Or, to quote Stillingfleet, 'as if everyone who rejects their pretence of infallibility had nothing to guide him but his own private fancy in the interpretation of Scripture' (*op. cit.,* p.181). Nothing could be further from the truth. Protestant exegesis from Luther and Calvin downward has played careful attention to the *consensus fidelium* (the consensus of believers) and has been profoundly suspicious of interpretations which bore the mark of novelty and idiosyncrasy. In fact, to a very substantial degree the Reformation itself was an appeal to what Stillingfleet called 'this universal sense of the Christian Church' against the sectarian and divisive exegesis of Rome and the Schoolmen. In every matter in dispute, argued the Reformers, it was the Protestant case which could claim the support of the Fathers. Whether they were right or wrong in making such a claim is not the issue. The point is that they regarded the task of biblical interpretation as a social and ecclesiatical one. It had to be done in the church and with the church. That is true still. The work of the great Protestant exegetes (and particularly those from the Anglican tradition) is massively indebted to the Fathers; and we enrich rather than impoverish such a hermeneutic by extending the consultation to include Reformers and Puritans. If the moment were opportune, we might even argue that it is the Roman Catholic Church which has lost contact with the *consensus fidelium*. The dogmatics of Trent present an insuperable barrier to any meaningful interaction with the best hermeneutical traditions of Christendom.

OBSTACLES

There are good reasons for doubting whether the ARCIC proposals will ever be implemented. At least three major obstacles stand in the way: the implications for the monarchy; the loose, trans-national character of Anglicanism; and the problem of women's ordination.

The Monarchy

The most remarkable feature of the documents produced by ARCIC is their total silence with regard to Her Majesty the Queen. Henry VIII transferred to himself all the prerogatives previously enjoyed by the papacy and this was reaffirmed by the Elizabethan Settlement, according to which the Sovereign enjoys ecclesiastical as well as political supremacy in England. In effect, she is Head of the Anglican Church and all her clergy forswear loyalty to any foreign jurisdiction. In addition, the Sovereign, in her Coronation Oath, vows to maintain the Protestant Reformed religion and the doctrine, worship and discipline of the Church of England. It is true, of course, that presbyterians could never accept the idea of the Royal Supremacy over the Church; and true, too, that it is far from clear what it actually means. But the point that matters for the moment is that the constitutional implications of the ARCIC proposals are extremely grave. The Queen would cease to be Head of the Church; she would cease to be Protestant; and she would cease to have any constitutional right to the Crown. She would also forfeit the allegiance of what is probably the most solidly Royalist group in the country: the Evangelical Protestant community. When one adds to these the further consideration that the ARCIC proposals would have profound repercussions in Ulster one can only marvel that the question of the Sovereign's position has been so completely ignored. The failure to consult her is a grave insult to Her Majesty; and it casts serious doubts on the wisdom and integrity of the negotiators.

International Anglicanism

The very loose international structures of Anglicanism mean that whatever Canterbury may decide there is no guarantee that other provinces will follow its lead. The members of ARCIC seem to believe that the Archbishop of Canterbury has a position analogous to that of the Pope: 'Anglicanism,' we are told, 'has never rejected the principle and practice of primacy. New reflection upon it has been stimulated by the evolving role of the Archbishop of Canterbury within the Anglican Communion. The development of this form of primacy arose precisely from the need for a service of unity in the faith in an expanding communion of churches. It finds expression in the Lambeth Conferences which originated with requests from overseas provinces for guidance in matters of faith. This illustrates a particular relationship between conciliarity and primacy in the Anglican Communion' (*The First Report*, p.77).

But this is a misunderstanding. The Archbishop of Canterbury is no Pope and the Lambeth conference is no Vatican Council. This was one of the points emphasised by Dr Gareth Bennet in his fateful Preface to *Crockford's Clerical Directory 1987/88:* 'The real fact is that there is a loose association of independent national churches with some weak consultative bodies which attempt to ensure agreement in faith and order and advise on common action' (p.64). As for the Archbishop of Canterbury, writes Dr Bennett, it is 'less than realistic to ignore his actual powerlessness..... He has no right to interfere in any province's internal affairs; he can advise and warn but his worldwide journeys have the disadvantage that everywhere he goes he is an honoured guest' (p.65). The General Synod, equally, lacks overall authority: 'For the most part the synod is virtually powerless and consistently ineffective. Its strings are pulled from elsewhere. It finds itself faced with a government of the Church which is almost independent of it. The irritation which many bishops feel at having to spend so much time at Synod meetings, and their desultory contributions to its debates, is founded on the knowledge that nothing the Synod does has much effect on them, the administration of their diocese or the work of the leadership group within it' p.69).

It is clear from this that Anglicanism has never accepted the principle of primacy as understood in Roman Catholicism and it has certainly never known it in practice. There is not one Anglican church but several (the impression that there is 'a single church of which the provinces are sub-divisions' is entirely false, according to Bennet). It is extremely unlikely that any decision by Canterbury or the General Synod to unite with Rome under the primacy of the Pope would command the assent of other provinces. The same applies to decisions of the Lambeth Conference, international though that gathering is. The Province of New South Wales (under Archbishop Donald Robinson) and especially the Diocese of Sydney would almost certainly refuse to follow Canterbury in such a move.

The Ordination of Women

The problems over the identity and coherence of Anglicanism have been dramatically highlighted by the debate on the admission of women to the ordained priesthood. The problem first arose in 1971 when it was agreed to allow the small province of Hong Kong, because of its special circumstances, to ordain women. In July, 1974, there was an ordination of eleven women in the Episcopal Church in Philadelphia, USA. The American House of Bishops later declared these ordinations invalid but in the General Conventions at Minneapolis in 1976 a motion that women should be eligible for all three forms of ministry was passed by a slender majority. In the meantime, the General Synod of the Anglican Church in Canada gave approval in principle to the ordination of women. And in July, 1975, Archbishop Donald Coggan sent a letter to Pope Paul VI which included the following paragraph: 'We write now to inform Your Holiness of the slow but steady growth of a consensus of opinion within the Anglican Communion that there are no fundamental objections in principle to the ordination of women to the priesthood.'

The movement towards the ordination of women

has obviously gathered considerable momentum. Indeed, it is now virtually unstoppable. But the agitation has brought its own problems. For one thing, it has led to strained relations between the various provinces of the Anglican Communion. Those which already ordain women berate those which don't and accuse them of dragging their heels; and those which still have no women priests accuse those which have of going ahead without proper consultation. The problem becomes particularly embarrassing when women priests from overseas come to Britain and find themselves unrecognised and unable to officiate.

But there have also been problems in relations between the bishops themselves: problems which will be greatly exacerbated when the first woman bishop is consecrated, probably in the not too distant future. The Bishop of London, Dr Graham Leonard, has already become embroiled in controversy over the issue by taking under his own episcopal care an American priest and congregation who were expelled from the Episcopal Church for refusing to acquiesce in the ordination of women. Dr Leonard has also let it be known that he would regard a unilateral decision by Anglicanism to ordain women as a breach of Catholic order so grave as to dissolve the terms of communion. In other words, he would feel bound to leave the Church of England.

It is in the area of Anglican-Roman Catholic dialogue, however, that proposals to ordain women would have the most dramatic effects. Dr Bennet comments (page 67): 'There is no doubt that this new question about Anglican orders would be a setback which some would regard as irretrievable.' This is certainly how Roman Catholicism sees the situation.

Responding to the Archbishop of Canterbury's letter of July 1975 Pope Paul VI wrote:

'Your Grace is of course well aware of the Catholic Church's position on this question. She holds that it is not admissible to ordain women to the priesthood for very fundamental reasons.... We must regretfully recognise that a new course taken by the Anglican Communion in admitting women to the ordained priesthood cannot fail to introduce into this dialogue an element of grave difficulty which those involved will have to take seriously into account.' In a later letter (written in March 1976) he spoke of 'the sadness with which we encounter so grave a new obstacle and threat'.

Catholic Objections

On this issue the sympathies of most Conservative Evangelicals will lie with the Roman Catholics. The New Testament categorically excludes women from the ministry of teaching and ruling the church (1 Tim. 2.12) and it is very difficult to see how anyone can seriously take the Bible as his rule of faith (the hall-mark of evangelicalism) and go on to disregard its unambiguous teaching in this area.

But the discussion merits a slightly more thorough survey. Official Roman Catholic thinking on this subject is conveniently summarised in the Declaration *Inter Insigniores* issued by the Sacred Congregation for the Doctrine of the Faith in 1976. The Sacred Congregation also issued an Official Commentary on *Inter Insigniores*. Both these documents, along with relevant correspondence between Rome and

Canterbury, were published by the Catholic Truth Society under the title *Women Priests: Obstacle to Unity?* (1986. Page references in the following quotations are from this source). To their credit, these documents frankly recognise that down through the centuries women have suffered exploitation and repression. There is abundant evidence of prejudice against women even in Christian sources, such as the writings of the early Fathers. But the problem is by no means confined to the past. The *Official Commentary on Inter Insigniores* concludes by saying, 'We still have a long way to go before all the inequalities of which women are still the victims are eliminated, not only in the field of public, professional and intellectual life, but even within the family.' (page 45).

The Sacred Congregation also acknowledge the value of the contribution made by women to the life of the church. Some have left writings so rich in spiritual content 'that Pope Paul VI has included them among the Doctors of the Church' (page 4). On the day of Pentecost the Spirit filled *all* the disciples, women as well as men. And both the Acts of the Apostles and the Epistles of Paul stress the role of women in evangelising, instructing new converts and even in prophesying.

Roman Catholicism is also sensitive to the changing role of women in society and to the ever-growing influence of international feminism, reflected in such an event as International Woman's Year (1975) (in which the Holy See took part). The Second Vatican Council had already caught the mood: 'Since in our times women have an ever more active share in the whole life of society, it is very important that they participate more widely also in the various fields of the Church's apostolate.'

For an institution as skilled in marketing as the Roman Catholic Church the temptation to fall in with the spirit of the age must be a strong one. Yet it remains adamantly opposed to the ordination of women: 'By calling only men to the priestly Order and ministry in its true sense, the Church intends to remain faithful to the type of ordained ministry willed by the Lord Jesus Christ and carefully maintained by the Apostles' (page 6).

Many of the arguments used to support this position commend themselves immediately to Conservative Evangelicals.

First, there is 'the remarkable fact that Jesus did not entrust the apostolic charge to women'. This cannot be dismissed as merely a matter of conforming to the customs of the time: 'His attitude towards women was quite different from that of His milieu and He deliberately and courageously broke with it' (as He did, of course, on many other issues).

Secondly, there is the practice of the apostles. There was never any suggestion of their ordaining women nor of extending to them the official and public proclamation of the message. In fact, as we have seen, they explicitly forbade such a step (1 Tim. 2). This does not mean that the apostles, any more than their Lord, were culture-bound. They had no scruples whatever about breaking with Mosaic practices when that was called for 'and they could therefore have envisaged conferring ordination on women, if they had not been convinced of their duty of fidelity to the Lord on this point' (page 8). Besides, many of the surrounding religions had priestesses, and it would have given no offence for the church to have the same.

In fact, far from suggesting that the apostles were misogynists the New Testament documents reflect a remarkably positive attitude towards women. In the final salutations of his letters Paul refers to many women who had been his co-workers. Some, like Priscilla, had an important influence on the emerging leadership of the church. Others, like Phoebe, spent their lives in its service. And yet others, like Lydia, were clearly women of substance. These women were not characterless chattels. They were strong, gifted, spiritual personalities, no doubt drawing inspiration and encouragement from the affirmation of the fundamental equality of men and women which we find in Gal. 3.28: 'There is neither Jew nor Greek, there is neither bond nor free, there is neither male nor female: for you are all one in Christ Jesus.'

Such arguments, firmly based on the Bible, Evangelicals can applaud. But at other points the Vatican arguments are curious, to say the least. They take us right out of the biblical grid and into the very different world of Roman Catholic ecclesiology and sacramentalism.

This appears first of all in the importance attached to tradition. Any corresponding Protestant study would probably include most of the material gathered under this heading in *Inter Insigniores,* but it would not be regarded as authoritative. It would represent only a history of opinion on the subject, stimulating ideas and creating confidence (by its unanimity) that the ordination of women is simply sectarian. The Sacred Congregation use this material differently. For them, it is the point of departure, to be consulted before scripture. More disturbingly, in the course of using the tradition, *Inter Insigniores* is at pains to insist that the teaching of the New Testament itself is not sufficient to settle the issue. 'This brings us to the fundamental observation,' says the Sacred Congregation at one point: 'We must not expect the New Testament *on its own* to resolve in a clear fashion the question of the possibility of women acceding to the priesthood, in the same way that it does not on its own enable us to give an account of certain sacraments, and especially of the structure of the sacrament of order' (page 30). Similar sentiments are expressed a few pages later: 'It must be repeated that the texts of the New Testament, even on such points as the sacraments, do not always give all the light that one could wish to find in them. Unless the value of unwritten traditions is admitted, it is sometimes difficult to discover in scripture entirely explicit indications of Christ's will' (page 33).

Here we are back to the old problem, authority, and to the endemic concern of Catholic theologians to harp on the theme of the inadequacy and opaqueness of the scriptures. We have already seen Knox and Bullough use this technique as a prelude to introducing the need for unwritten traditions. Not suprisingly, *Inter Insigniores* quickly appeals to the infallibility of the church: 'How are we to interpret the constant and universal practice of the Church? A theologian is certain that what the Church does she can in fact do, since she has the assistance of the Holy Spirit. This is a classical argument found again and again in St Thomas with regard to the sacraments' (page 25).

This says, presumably without blushing, that something is right simply because the church has always done it (or thought it and taught it) and that something is wrong because the church has never done it. A Protestant can only blink. Which church are we talking about? What about a dogma such as the Immaculate Conception which St Thomas not only did not teach but emphatically denied? And what of the Assumption of the Virgin, a novelty unknown even to 'the Church' until the 20th century? Does infallibility mean that the church can declare something to be true when it lacks the support not only of scripture but even of tradition itself? This certainly happened in connection with the Marian dogmas, which, as Dr. A. N. S. Lane points out, represent 'not so much an appeal to tradition as the triumph of dogma over tradition' (*New Dictionary of Theology*, P. 416).

Ministry and Order

The argument is also put forward that the ordination of women has taken place only in churches which have rejected the concept of Order: 'It is very enlightening to note that the communities springing from the Reformation which have had no difficulty in giving women access to the pastoral office are first and foremost those that have rejected the Catholic doctrine on the sacrament of order and profess that the pastor is only one baptised person among others, even if the charge given has been the object of consecration' (page 39).

The first response to this must be that Protestantism is certainly unhappy with some aspects of the idea of ordination. The word did not come into ecclesiology from the New Testament. It came from the Latin *ordo,* which was primarily a military term meaning *rank*. There is little doubt that it has contributed significantly to the problem of clericalism in the church, suggesting both that there is a sharp distinction between people (laity) and clergy and that within the clergy itself there is a graduated, military-type structure from priest to bishop, archbishop, cardinal and Pope. Such ideas run totally counter to the New Testament emphasis on the priesthood of all believers, according to which all Christians have received the Holy Spirit, all possess charismata and all are called to ministry. In the New Testament, everyone has his own office (Latin *officium,* duty) and every child of God is his own priest, making his own confession, offering his own sacrifice of gratitude and coming right up to the Throne with his own prayers.

On the other hand, the historic Protestant churches have always insisted on *order* and on a high view of 'the ministry'. It is a complete misunderstanding to see presbyterianism, for example, as simply a form of democracy. The rights of the people have indeed been carefully safeguarded, especially in the sense that no elder or minister could be imposed on congregations against their wishes. But presbyterian elders are not simply tribunes of the people. They are authority figures. Even though their position is one of service rather than rank their service itself implied that they were *over* the church. Furthermore, in The New Testament it was the Holy Spirit (Acts 20.28) not the people, who called them: and He called them to *oversight*. They were to lead, teach, counsel and admonish: all of them authority-functions. The gifts for these ministries came from God, as did the 'leading' by which the church came to appoint specific individuals to the work.

The Protestant churches retained the view that the ministry was a specific vocation, that it required arduous spiritual and intellectual preparation and that admission to it should be marked by a special solemn service of consecration. First-generation Reformers such as Calvin and Knox discontinued the practice of laying-on hands, partly because of its association with what they regarded as the indefensible views of Catholicism and partly because of the problems involved in the new Testament references to the practice. These problems are still unsolved, as can be seen in Schweizer's *Church Order in the New Testament,* especially p. 206ff. For example, in Acts 13.3 Paul and Barnabas were set aside by the laying on of hands, even although they were already prophets and although Paul would vehemently deny that it was to any such act he owed his apostleship (Gal. 1.12). The laying-on of hands here marked consecration to a new sphere of service, not admission to an office or promotion to a higher rank); and if the church today were to base its practice on Acts 13.3 there would be a laying-on of hands every time a man moved to a new work. Notwithstanding these difficulties, however, later generations of Protestants reinstated the practice of ordination by laying-on of hands so that it can at least be said that the ceremony by which we admit to this 'good work' (1 Tim. 3.1) testifies to a high view of its dignity and yields nothing in solemnity to its Roman Catholic counterpart. There are indeed signs today that clear ideas on church order are at a discount. Self-appointed prophets and apostles abound. But such a trend cannot claim the sanction of either the New Testament or the Protestant tradition.

But the real problem is not that Roman Catholicism wants *order* while Protestantism decries it but that the former has a very peculiar idea of what is conferred by ordination. According to Ott, (*op. cit.,* P. 450ff.) ordination is a sacrament (*The Sacrament of Holy Order*) which confers a special priestly status, essentially different from the 'lay state'. Like all other sacraments (in the Roman view) Holy Order has an invariable, almost mechanical, efficacy. It does three things: it confers sanctifying grace on the recipient; it imprints a character on the recipient; and it confers a permanent spiritual power on the recipient. It is this last which really matters in connection with the problem of women's ordination. The spiritual power spoken of is connected primarily with the Eucharist. The priest receives the power of consecrating and offering the Eucharistic sacrifice. This means particularly that by simply uttering the words of institution ('This is my body') the priest effects the transformation of the sacramental bread into the body, soul and divinity of Jesus Christ. Rome does not hesitate to carry this to its logical conclusion. The officiating priest is doing exactly what Christ did on Calvary: 'In virtue of the man's ordination he shares in Christ's great priestly act, the consecration of His own body and blood at the offering of His own great sacrifice: the offering which He commanded His friends to do in remembrance of Him, and which the priest obediently performs when he celebrates Mass' (Bullough, *Op. Cit.,* p. 115).

This concept of the priesthood clearly (and of course, inevitably) underlies *Inter Insigniores* and the related documents on the ordination of women: 'The bishop or the priest, in the exercise of his ministry, does not act in his own name, *in persona propria*: he represents Christ, who acts through him' (page 12); '"The priest enacts the image of Christ, in whose person and by whose power he pronounces the words of consecration" (St Thomas)'. ARCIC fully shares this view: there is no hint that the Anglican participants demurred. We read, for example: 'The ordained ministry is called priestly principally because it has a particular sacramental relationship with Christ as High Priest. At the Eucharist Christ's people do what He commanded in memory of Himself and Christ unites them sacramentally with Himself in His self-offering. But in this action it is only the ordained minister who presides at the Eucharist, in which, in the name of Christ and on behalf of His Church, He recites the narrative of the institution of the Lord's Supper, and invokes the Holy Spirit upon the gifts' (page 41).

Protestantism has always argued that such views of the ministry and the sacraments are completely unscriptural and therefore to be rejected. In fact, Roman Catholicism itself would hardly dare argue that these ideas can be found in the New Testament. Such evidence as does exist comes only from later phases of tradition, as *The Final Report* itself concedes: 'Despite the fact that in the New Testament ministers are never called "priests" (*hiereis*), Christians came to see the priestly role of Christ reflected in these ministers and used priestly terms in describing them' (page 35).

But what has all this to do with the ordination of women? It is very difficult to see anything in womanhood as such to disable them from pronouncing the words of consecration with the same power and effect as males. The crucial point in the Roman Catholic argument appears to be the idea of *representation*. The priest represents Christ, even to the extent of being personally a sacramental sign. Such a function could not be performed by a woman because this would contradict the idea of 'natural resemblance'. 'The same natural resemblance is required for persons as for things' says *Inter Insigniores:* 'When Christ's role in the Eucharist is to be expressed sacramentally, there would not be this "natural resemblance" which must exist between Christ and His minister if the role of Christ were not taken by a man: in such a case it would be difficult to see in the minister the image of Christ. For Christ Himself was and remains a man' (page 14). And in the *Official Commentary* we read: 'It is precisely because the priest is a sign of Christ the Saviour that He must be a man and not a woman' (page 39).

Such arguments serve only to lead Catholicism into a morass. The idea of 'natural resemblance' is foreign to both scripture and tradition. One hesitates to score cheap debating points. But it is very difficult to see any 'natural resemblance' between the Pope, robed in spendour and surrounded with pomp and circumstance, and the Christ who was crucified between two thieves on the town garbage-heap. It is even more difficult to see any 'natural resemblance' between a piece of bread and 'the body, soul and divinity' of the Lord Jesus Christ. Besides, the argument that if natural resemblance must involve sex, it must also involve race cannot be dismissed as easily as *Inter Insigniores* pretends. The natural representative of Christ, presumably, is a Jew; and the argument that Christ chose no Gentile apostle has, *a priori,* as much force as the argument that He chose no women. And what evidence is there, anyway, for the idea of a Christian minister being a representative of Christ? The only biblical support adduced for this idea is 2 Cor. 5.20: 'Now then we are ambassadors for Christ, as though God did beseech you by us: we pray you in Christ's stead, be reconciled to God.' The trouble with this is that what is true of an apostle is not necessarily true of a priest; otherwise we shall have to argue that not only the Pope but every member of the clergy is infallible. More important, representation here has nothing to do with the sacraments. Paul is not saying that as he presides at the Eucharist he is Christ's ambassador. He is saying that as he preaches the gospel he is Christ's ambassador. Unfortunately for the Catholic argument, it has already conceded that women may be prophets and even canonised as 'doctors': so that it has thrown the idea of natural resemblance out the window at the very point (proclamation) where its proof-text applies it.

All that is achieved by the elaborate argument of the Sacred Congregation is to burden the question of the ordination of women with all the extra difficulties inherent in the Roman Catholic doctrine of Holy Order. Every step in the argument is wobbly; the idea of the Eucharist as a sacrifice; the idea of ministers as priests; the idea of priests as representatives; and the idea of representation requiring a 'natural resemblance' to Christ Himself. So far as this last point is concerned, it is the lack of resemblance (the asymmetry) that the New Testament highlights: 'We have this treasure in earthen vessels' (2 Cor. 4.7).

The only safe course is to argue on biblical grounds: the example of Christ; the teaching and practice of the apostles; and the very serious arguments from basic theology which they (and especially Paul) present in support of their position (1 Tim. 2.12-15). Once we abandon such arguments we quickly find ourselves 'darkening counsel by words without knowledge' (Job 38.2). Or is it that Roman Catholicism cannot bring itself to base its case on the Bible alone?

The problem of women's ordination will, in all likelihood, eventually kill off the ARCIC proposals. In and of itself that will be a welcome development. But the way it comes about will bring sadness to the hearts of many who view the Church of England with affection. Christendom owes an immense debt to the many martyrs, saints and scholars who have graced Anglicanism. What a tragedy that its survival should now depend not on the inherent strength of its own principles and the convictions of its own clergy but on the scruples of its historical adversary.

By the same author

The Spirit of Promise

This book covers the work of the Holy Spirit

The chapter headings are:

1. **Baptism in the Spirit.**
2. **But . . .**
3. **Holy Spirit Baptism: Seven Easy Steps.?**
4. **Have Spiritual Gifts Ceased?**
5. **Is the Church Today Charismatic?**
6. **The Sealing of the Spirit.**
7. **Led by the Spirit.**
8. **The Reality of the Spirit's Ministry.**
9. **Go on being filled!**
10. **Can we be Reformed Pentecostals?**

This is a challenging work — essential reading for all concerned about the teaching and operation of the Holy Spirit.

ISBN 0 906 7 31 48 8

Printed and bound in Great Britain by
Cox & Wyman Ltd, Reading